FROM CRACK HOUSE TO CEO:

The Inspiring Story of Mike Lindell

Jose K. Cox

From Crack House to CEO

All rights reserved. No part of this publication may be reproduced, distributed, or transmitted in any form or by any means, including photocopying, recording, or other electronic or mechanical methods, without the prior written permission of the publisher, except in the case of brief quotations embodied in critical reviews and certain other noncommercial uses permitted by copyright law.

Copyright ©Jose K. Cox, 2023

From Crack House to CEO

TABLE OF CONTENTS

INTRODUCTION

CHAPTER 1: EARLY LIFE

1.1 Career

1.2 Education

CHAPTER 2: INITIAL BUSINESS ENDEAVORS

2.1 Establishing MyPillow

2.2 Product and Service

2.3 Advertising and marketing

CHAPTER 3: PERSONAL LIFE

3.1 Family and Relationship

3.2 Beliefs in Religion

3.3 Generosity

CONCLUSION

INTRODUCTION

American entrepreneur and philanthropist Mike Lindell. He is the company's creator and CEO. MyPillow sells pillows and other bedding items. A multimillion-dollar corporation, MyPillow sells its products in more than 40,000 locations across North America.

A well-known political activist and conspiracy theorist, Lindell is also. He is a well-known advocate for former American President Donald Trump. Lindell had a crucial part in supporting and funding Trump's efforts to reverse the outcome of the 2020 U.S. presidential election after he lost, spreading unfounded rumors of massive electoral fraud.

In his whole career, Lindell has generated controversy. He has drawn criticism for his personal life, political beliefs, and business methods. He is still a prosperous

From Crack House to CEO

businessman and a well-known personality in American society, nevertheless.

CHAPTER 1: EARLY LIFE

In 1961, Mike Lindell was created in Mankato, Minnesota. He was raised in Minnesota's Chaska and Carver cities. In his adolescent years, his gambling addiction started to take hold. After high school, he enrolled at the University of Minnesota, but he left after only a few months. Lindell started doing cocaine in his 20s and became addicted to it. This addiction worsened when he switched to crack cocaine in the 1990s.

The height of Lindell's addiction was in 2008. He was residing in a crack house and was homeless. He had lost both his family and his business in addition to everything else. One night, Lindell had a dream in which God instructed him to design a pillow to promote restful sleep. He got up and started building the MyPillow prototype.

From Crack House to CEO

Early in life, Lindell struggled with addiction. He was able to conquer his addiction, nevertheless, and launch a prosperous company. He is currently a well-known philanthropist and businessman.

1.1 Career

Both the pre-MyPillow and post-MyPillow periods of Mike Lindell's career can be clearly separated.

Prior to MyPillow
In Carver County, Minnesota, Lindell started a number of small enterprises in the 1980s, such as carpet cleaning, lunch trailers, and a few taverns and restaurants. In Las Vegas, he also attempted to generate money by working as a professional card counter.

However, Lindell lost everything when his crack cocaine addiction became unmanageable in the 1990s. In 2008, he was housed in a crack house and unemployed.

From Crack House to CEO

Career Post-MyPillow

In a dream he had in 2009, God instructed Lindell to design a pillow that would promote restful sleep. He got up and started building the MyPillow prototype.

In 2009, Lindell introduced MyPillow. At first, he distributed the pillows via direct mail and at trade events. He started presenting infomercials for MyPillow in 2012. The infomercials were a great hit, and MyPillow swiftly gained recognition as a well-known brand.

MyPillow has grown to be a multimillion-dollar business. It has a manufacturing site in Chaska, Minnesota, where it employs over 1,500 people.

Lindell is not just employed by MyPillow but is also a political activist and a conspiracist. He is a well-known advocate for former American President Donald Trump. Lindell had a crucial part in supporting and funding Trump's efforts to reverse the outcome of the 2020 U.S.

presidential election after he lost, spreading unfounded rumors of massive electoral fraud.

Throughout his entire career, Lindell has generated controversy. He has drawn criticism for his personal life, political beliefs, and business methods. He is still a prosperous businessman and a well-known personality in American society, nevertheless.

1.2 Education

In Chaska, Minnesota, Mike Lindell graduated from Chaska High School. His graduation was in 1979. He next enrolled at the University of Minnesota but left after only a few months.

Lindell has never received a college degree. However, Liberty University has awarded him an honorary Doctor of Business degree. He received the diploma in 2019.

From Crack House to CEO

According to Lindell, he dropped out of college because he had no interest in going to classes. He added that he thought his time was being wasted.

Lindell has recently made statements about the value of education. He has expressed remorse about not completing college and urges youngsters to continue their education.

Lindell has had entrepreneurial success despite not having a formal degree. He is the creator and CEO of the lucrative company MyPillow. A well-known political activist, too.

Lindell has drawn criticism for being uneducated from some quarters. Others have applauded him for his accomplishments despite his difficulties, though.

CHAPTER 2: INITIAL BUSINESS ENDEAVORS

Before starting MyPillow, Mike Lindell was involved in a number of early company endeavors. Here are a few illustrations:

After his sister's apartment flooded in the 1980s, Lindell decided to launch a carpet cleaning company. He was reiterating, "Wow, this would be a good business,' and I wasn't doing anything."

Lunch wagons: In the 1980s, Lindell also established a lunch cart business. He was motivated by the popularity of lunch wagons in California and believed that Minnesota would be a good place to sell them.

In the 1980s, Lindell owned a number of pubs and eateries in Carver County, Minnesota. He had trouble running the companies, though, and he eventually lost them.

Lindell also made an effort to become a successful card counter in Las Vegas. He had little success, though, and soon gave up trying.

Early business endeavors by Lindell weren't always successful. However, he was able to use the lessons he had learned to improve MyPillow because he had learned from his errors.

Early business ventures by Lindell also demonstrate that he is a risk-taking businessman. Despite having little experience, he is open to trying new things. His success with MyPillow can be attributed in large part to his entrepreneurial attitude.

2.1 Establishing MyPillow

In 2009, Mike Lindell founded MyPillow. After having a dream in which God instructed him to design a pillow that would improve peoples' sleep, he got the concept for the business.

From Crack House to CEO

At the time, Lindell was experiencing homelessness and addiction problems. He had lost both his family and his business in addition to everything else. But the dream gave him optimism, so he made the decision to begin developing MyPillow.

MyPillow's prototype was created by Lindell over the course of several months. Until he discovered a pillow that was cozy and supportive, he tried it with various materials and styles. Additionally, he created a brand-new kind of pillow stuffing that consists of microfibers woven into shredded foam.

In 2009, Lindell introduced MyPillow. At first, he distributed the pillows via direct mail and at trade events. He started presenting infomercials for MyPillow in 2012. The infomercials were a great hit, and MyPillow swiftly gained recognition as a well-known brand.

MyPillow has grown to be a multimillion-dollar business. It has a manufacturing site in Chaska, Minnesota, where it employs over 1,500 people. In the US and Canada, more than 40,000 stores sell MyPillow products.

From Crack House to CEO

MyPillow was founded by Lindell, and it is a wonderful tale of prosperity and atonement. In order to establish a prosperous business, he overcame his addiction and homelessness. He serves as an example for many people who are facing difficulties in their own lives.

Some of the elements that helped MyPillow succeed include the following:

MyPillow pillows are renowned for their comfort and support. High-quality product. According to Lindell, his pillows are made only from the best materials. aggressive marketing campaign Lindell has made significant investments in MyPillow's marketing and advertising. He has produced print ads, TV commercials, and infomercials. In order to market MyPillow, he has also worked with celebrities and social media influencers.

Model of direct-to-consumer sales: MyPillow initially offered its goods to customers by way of its website and direct mail promotions. Due to this, Lindell was able to avoid the substantial expenses involved in selling goods through shops.

Made in the USA: Pillows from MyPillow are produced here. Many customers who want to support American companies have found this to be appealing.

MyPillow was founded by Lindell, and his success will no doubt serve as an example for future businesspeople.

2.2 Product and Service

The firm that sells pillows, bedding, and other sleep accouterments is called MyPillow, and its founder and CEO is Mike Lindell. Products from MyPillow are well renowned for providing comfort and support, and there are over 40,000 locations selling them in the US and Canada.

The following is a list of some of the goods and services MyPillow provides:

From Crack House to CEO

Pillows

The first MyPillow pillow is the MyPillow Classic. It is comprised of microfibers and shreds of foam that have been intertwined, and it is intended to support and comfort the head and neck.

A more opulent iteration of the MyPillow Classic is the MyPillow Premium. It is constructed from better-quality components and has a longer lifespan.

A more compact version of the MyPillow Classic that is ideal for travel is the MyPillow Travel.

A long, rectangular pillow called a MyPillow Body is intended to support the full body.

A scaled-down version of the MyPillow Classic created specifically for kids is called MyPillow Kids.

Bedding

The MyPillow Mattress Topper is a supportive and comfortable memory foam mattress topper.

Bed linens from MyPillow: A range of bed linens produced from various materials, such as cotton, polyester, and bamboo.

The bedspreads and comforters available from MyPillow come in a range of colors, patterns, and materials.

MyPillow Blankets: A selection of blankets constructed from various materials, such as fleece, cotton, and microfiber.

Additional Sleep Accessories

MyPillow Slippers: A selection of slippers in a range of styles and materials.

A selection of eye masks from MyPillow that are intended to block out light and encourage sleep.

MyPillow Ear Plugs: A selection of earplugs made to reduce noise and encourage sleep.

MyPillow Aromatherapy offers a range of aromatherapy items that are intended to encourage rest and sleep.

Additionally, MyPillow provides a range of services, such as:

* All items come with free shipping and returns * On all products, a 60-day money-back guarantee There is a 10-year warranty on all goods.

To give its customers the finest sleep experience possible, MyPillow is dedicated. The business provides a variety of goods and services to promote restful sleep and wakefulness.

2.3 Advertising and marketing

For his aggressive marketing and advertising efforts for MyPillow, Mike Lindell is well-known. He has made significant investments in print ads, TV commercials, and infomercials. In order to market MyPillow, he has also worked with celebrities and social media influencers.

Particularly well-known infomercials are those from Lindell. They are usually lengthy and include testimonies from Lindell regarding the advantages of MyPillow. During the infomercials, he also provides viewers with exclusive discounts and incentives to buy MyPillow items.

The television ads for Lindell are likewise quite powerful. They highlight clients that utilized MyPillow and had great outcomes. The end of the commercials sometimes includes a call to action urging viewers to buy MyPillow items.

To further market MyPillow, Lindell has teamed up with a variety of celebrities and social media influencers. He has paid them to promote MyPillow items in interviews and on their social media pages. This has made it easier for Lindell to reach more people and spark interest in the MyPillow goods.

The marketing and advertising campaign for Lindell has been quite effective. MyPillow has grown into a multimillion-dollar business with items available in more than 40,000 locations across North America.

From Crack House to CEO

The following are some of the most important components of Lindell's marketing and advertising plan:

1. Benefit-focused marketing and advertising Lindell's marketing and advertising materials emphasize the advantages of utilizing MyPillow goods, such as greater sleep, less neck pain, and better general health.
2. Make use of endorsements: Lindell frequently includes customer endorsements in his marketing and advertising materials. This encourages potential customers to trust MyPillow and persuades them that its products work.
3. Provide exclusive discounts and incentives: Lindell frequently provides exclusive discounts and incentives for MyPillow purchases. This increases the products' accessibility and appeal to prospective clients.
4. Work with celebrities and social media influencers to market MyPillow products. Lindell has collaborated with a number of celebrities and influencers on social media. This makes it easier for him to reach more people and spark interest in the MyPillow products.

From Crack House to CEO

The marketing and advertising plan employed by Lindell is a good illustration of how to market a product successfully. He emphasizes the advantages of the product, employs endorsements, provides special deals and incentives, and collaborates with well-known people and social media influencers. With the aid of this tactic, he was able to establish a prosperous company and give MyPillow a well-known brand name.

CHAPTER 3: PERSONAL LIFE

Mike Lindell has seen both success and hardship in his personal life. He overcame drugs and destitution to start a prosperous company, but he has also gotten into some hot water.

In 1961, Lindell was born in Mankato, Minnesota. He was raised in a working-class household. His father was a carpenter, and his mother was a stay-at-home mom.

When Lindell was a teenager, he started gambling. He gambled away a lot of his money, which led to debt. Lindell developed a crack cocaine addiction in the 1990s. His addiction gradually got out of hand, costing him everything. In 2008, he was housed in a crack house and unemployed.

From Crack House to CEO

Lindell made the decision to seek addiction treatment in 2008. After entering rehab, he achieved sobriety. He also began developing MyPillow.

MyPillow soon achieved commercial success. Now a multimillionaire, Lindell is referred to as the "My Pillow Guy."

A well-known political activist, Lindell is also. He is a well-known advocate for former American President Donald Trump. Lindell had a crucial part in supporting and funding Trump's efforts to reverse the outcome of the 2020 U.S. presidential election after he lost, spreading unfounded rumors of massive electoral fraud.

Throughout his entire career, Lindell has generated controversy. He has drawn criticism for his personal life, political beliefs, and business methods. He is still a prosperous businessman and a well-known personality in American society, nevertheless.

3.1 Family and Relationship

Mike Lindell has children from his first marriage and has been married twice. After roughly 20 years, his first marriage terminated in divorce. Dallas Yocum, whom he married in June 2013, left him, and they filed for divorce in the middle of July. According to Lindell, they had a prenuptial agreement.

According to a 2021 Daily Mail article, Lindell dated Jane Krakowski for nine months between the end of 2019 and the summer of 2020. Both Krakowski and Lindell refuted the charge. Lindell filed a lawsuit against the Daily Mail, alleging libel, with counsel Charles Harder.

Lindell has maintained a largely discreet family life. His children's names and ages remain a secret. Additionally, he has avoided discussing his romance with Krakowski in the media.

From Crack House to CEO

It is evident that Lindell has placed a high value on his family and relationships. He has, however, also opted to keep many of these particulars a secret.

3.2 Beliefs in Religion

An evangelical Christian, Mike Lindell. He has spoken about his faith and how it has influenced his life in front of the public. He has acknowledged that he gives God the glory for both his professional accomplishments and his battle with addiction.

A private, evangelical Christian university in Lynchburg, Virginia called Liberty University awarded Lindell an honorary doctorate in business in 2019. During the convocation, Liberty University President Jerry Falwell Jr. said of Lindell that he was "one of the greatest Christian businessmen on the planet.

Lindell has also taken part in a variety of Christian projects. He established the non-profit Lindell

Foundation, which helps former addicts obtain treatment and other services. He also supports the Union Gospel Mission and the Salvation Army.

Religious convictions have had a big impact on Lindell's life and career. He has claimed that he is inspired to help people and promote the gospel by a desire to do so.

Examples of how Lindell's religious convictions have affected his life and career include the following:

According to Lindell, he founded MyPillow because he felt compelled to do so by God. Additionally, he has stated that he gives up a portion of MyPillow's earnings to Christian charity. Lindell has emphasized the value of religion in the workplace. According to him, he encourages his staff to pray and read the Bible. In addition, Lindell has participated in a number of political activities driven by his religious convictions. For instance, he has backed legislation that would make it harder to get an abortion.

Both admiration and disapproval have been expressed for Lindell's religious views. Some people respect his dedication to his faith and his desire to spread it to others. His use of his platform to advance his religious beliefs has drawn criticism from others.

Whatever one's opinion of Lindell's religious convictions, it is certain that they have had a significant impact on both his life and his work.

3.3 Generosity

Millions of dollars have been contributed by philanthropist Mike Lindell to numerous charities and organizations. He established the non-profit Lindell Foundation, which helps former addicts obtain treatment and other services. He also supports the Union Gospel Mission and the Salvation Army.

In addition to helping those who are homeless and recovering from addiction, Lindell has donated to organizations that help children, veterans, and other vulnerable groups. He has contributed to organizations like the Children's Miracle Network, Teen Challenge, and the Wounded Warrior Project, for instance.

Additionally, Lindell has contributed to numerous relief operations during natural disasters. He gave blankets and pillows to Hurricane Harvey victims in 2017. In 2018, he gave pillows to California wildfire victims.

His Christian convictions serve as the basis for Lindell's philanthropy. He has asserted that he thinks Christians are called to serve others and change the world.

Here are some particular instances of Lindell's generosity:

In order to help the Salvation Army's programs for addiction rehabilitation, Lindell gave $1 million to the organization in 2017. 2018 saw Lindell provide $1 million to Union Gospel Mission in order to fund its outreach initiatives for the homeless. In order to support

From Crack House to CEO

the Wounded Warrior Project's activities for veterans and their families in 2019, Lindell gave $1 million to the organization. Lindell gave the Children's Miracle Network $1 million in 2020 to assist its hospitals and initiatives for kids with disabilities.

Numerous people's lives have been significantly impacted by Lindell's philanthropy. He has supported homeless people, veterans, kids, and other disadvantaged groups in their efforts to recover from addiction. Many people who want to change the world look up to him as an inspiration.

CONCLUSION

Mike Lindell is a complicated and divisive individual. He is an activist in politics as well as a wealthy businessman. Additionally, he is a conspiracy theorist who has circulated unfounded allegations of voter fraud.

The debate about Lindell's legacy is likely to persist for many years. Some people will remember him for his altruism and commercial achievement. Others will recall him for his divisive political beliefs and advocacy of conspiracies.

Whatever his legacy, Lindell will always be a prominent figure in American culture. He is a self-made businessman who has had considerable success. He is a fierce supporter of his causes.

Made in the USA
Columbia, SC
12 April 2025